Contents

Some words are shown in bold, **like this**. You can find out what they mean by looking in the glossary.

What Is a Mushroom?

This mass of mushrooms is growing at the bottom of an old tree.

A mushroom is a kind of **fungus**. A fungus is like a plant but it has no green leaves.

Spore

Growing underground

Button mushrooms

Field mushrooms are one of the few kinds of mushroom that you can eat.

There are thousands of different kinds of fungi. This book is about field mushrooms.

A Small Beginning

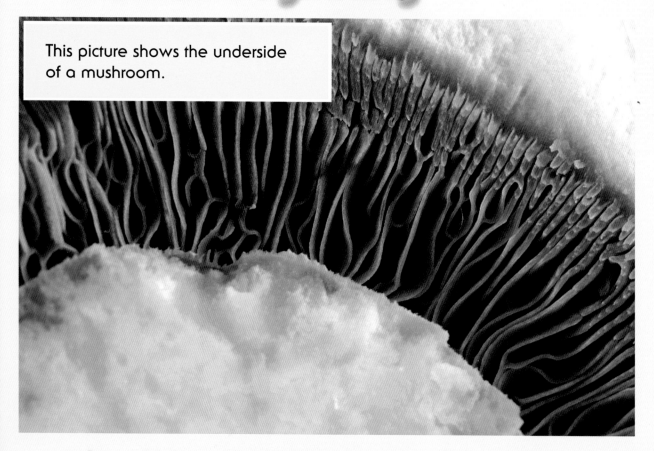

This picture shows the underside of a mushroom.

Like all kinds of **fungi**, mushrooms begin life as tiny **spores** in the fall. The spores grow on the underside of the parent mushroom.

Spore

Growing underground

Button mushrooms

A damp, grassy field is a good place for field mushrooms to grow.

Millions of spores blow away from the parent mushroom. Some of the spores land on moist **soil**.

Growing in the field

Ripe mushrooms

5 years

Growing Underground

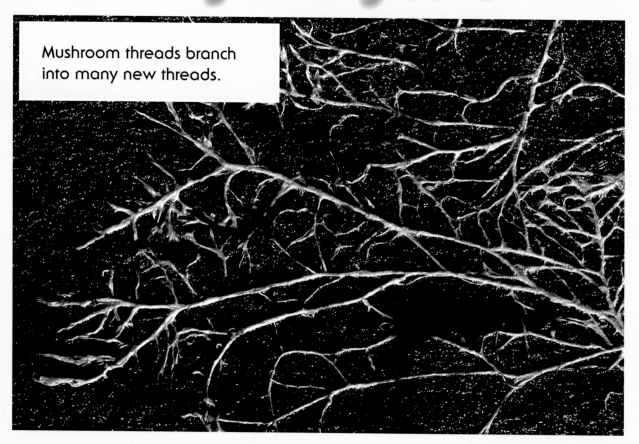

Mushroom threads branch into many new threads.

A tiny **thread** grows out from the **spore**. The thread grows longer and longer.

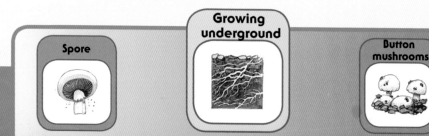

Spore

Growing underground

Button mushrooms

Mushroom threads can cover
a wide area underground.

The threads take in food and water from the **soil**. Some threads join together with threads from other spores.

The Next 12 Months

Warm, damp soil helps the mushroom grow.

In late summer, the **soil** is warm and damp. A small mushroom begins to grow underground on part of the web of **threads**.

Spore

Growing underground

Button mushrooms

Other mushrooms are growing, too. They live on the food and water taken in by the threads.

The mushrooms look like buttons when they are small.

Growing in the field

Ripe mushrooms

5 years

Growing in the Field

cap

The caps of these mushrooms are still closed.

stalk

As the mushrooms grow bigger, the **stalks** push up through the **soil**. The top of the mushroom is called the cap.

Spore

Growing underground

Button mushrooms

The open cap looks like an umbrella.

ring

The mushroom cap opens up. There is a ring of thin skin where the cap was joined to the stalk.

Growing in the field

Ripe mushrooms

5 years

Food for Animals

Foxes love mushrooms.

Pigs, mice, and other animals eat some of the mushrooms.

Spore

Growing underground

Button mushrooms

A fox can smell mushrooms in a field.

When a fox smells the mushrooms, it picks one or two and chews them up.

Growing in the field

Ripe mushrooms

5 years

Next Day

In some places you can find many different mushrooms for sale.

People like to eat mushrooms, too. You can buy mushrooms in a grocery store or at a farmers' market.

Spore

Growing underground

Button mushrooms

This woman is a mushroom **expert**. She knows which mushrooms are safe to pick. Some **wild** mushrooms are **poisonous**.

Only experts should pick mushrooms in the wild.

New Spores

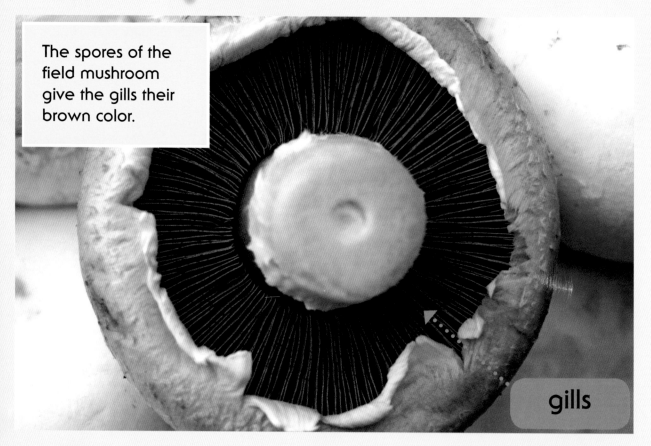

The spores of the field mushroom give the gills their brown color.

gills

The underside of the mushroom cap is covered with thin ridges called **gills**. The gills are covered with millions of **spores**.

Spore

Growing underground

Button mushrooms

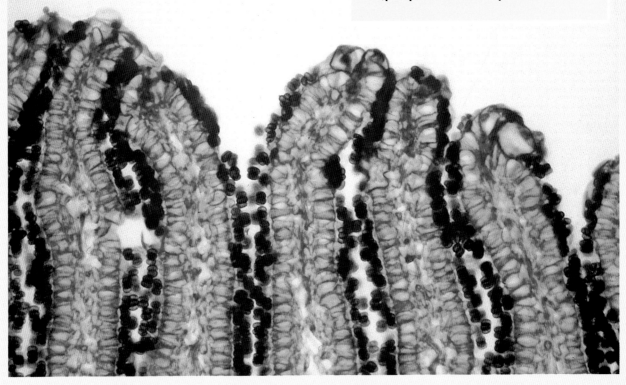

This picture is a close-up of gill cells (blue) and spores (purple-brown spots).

The tiny building blocks of living things are called cells. Spores are made inside special cells along a mushroom's gills.

Growing in the field

Ripe mushrooms

5 years

1 Day Later

After the spores are carried away in the wind, the mushroom dies.

Sometimes the wind can blow **spores** a long way. Some spores from the field mushroom ended up in the forest.

Spore

Growing underground

Button mushrooms

Many kinds of **fungi** grow in the forest. But the **soil** in the forest is not right for the field mushroom. Its spores will not grow there.

This honey fungus grows in the forest.

Growing in the field

Ripe mushrooms

5 years

1 Year Later

Some field mushroom **spores** fell in this meadow. They grew and made new mushrooms.

Field mushrooms grow in wet grasslands.

Spore

Growing underground

Button mushrooms

The white mushroom caps are easy to see in the grass.

In late summer the new mushrooms pushed up through the ground.

Growing in the field

Ripe mushrooms

5 years

5 Years Later

These field mushrooms have spread out to make a "fairy ring."

Every year the underground **threads** grow to make new mushrooms.

Spore

Growing underground

Button mushrooms

This tractor is plowing a field.

When a tractor breaks up the **soil** and turns it over, the threads of all the **fungi** are broken, too.

Growing in the field

Ripe mushrooms

5 years

A Mushroom Farm

Mushrooms do not need light to grow.

Most of the mushrooms we eat are grown on special mushroom farms.

Spore

Growing underground

Button mushrooms

These mushrooms are growing in underground caves.

New mushrooms can grow all the time in damp places.

Growing in the field

Ripe mushrooms

5 years

Life Cycle

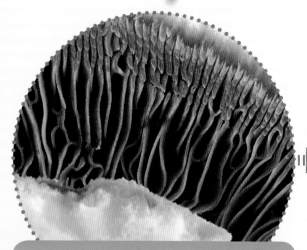

Spores

Growing underground

Button mushrooms

Ripe mushrooms

5 years later

Fact File

-  There are about 3,300 different kinds of mushrooms.

- Each mushroom produces up to 40 million **spores** every hour for about two days. Only a few of these will grow into new mushrooms.

- A few kinds of mushrooms are so **poisonous** they can kill you if you eat them, so do not pick **wild** mushrooms.

- Long ago, people used to think that "fairy rings" were made by fairies dancing. They thought that the mushrooms were seats the fairies sat on to rest.

Glossary

expert   someone who knows a lot about something

fungus (**fungi** for more than one) a living thing that is like a plant, but which cannot make food for itself the way that green plants can

gills   the soft brown underside of a mushroom cap

poisonous   able to cause illness or death if eaten

soil   the layer of mud that covers much of the land

spore   part of a mushroom that can grow into new fungi

stalk   stem that joins the cap of a mushroom to its underground threads

thread   fine strand, like a hair

wild   growing or living without the help of people

More Books to Read

Royston, Angela. *Looking at Life Cycles: How Do Plants and Animals Change?* Berkeley Heights, NJ: Enslow Elementary, 2008.

Spilsbury, Louise and Richard. *World of Plants: How Do Plants Grow?* Chicago: Heinemann Library, 2006.

Index